Sharpening Hand Tools

by Max Alth

No doubt, the hammer was the first tool invented. Somehow, early man found that it was better to hammer things with a rock in his hand than with his fist alone, and the hammer was discovered. Later, man found that it was better still to fasten the stone to a handle, and the true hammer was born.

The sharpened edge was probably the second tool invented. One can knock a saber-toothed tiger to the ground with a hammer, but one cannot use a hammer to cut tiger steaks. At first, naturally sharp-edged shards of hard stones, such as flint and obsidian, were used for cutting. As the years went by, someone thought of putting edges on the stones, and man began to chip and knap (pressure chip). After only a few hundred thousand years, someone came up with the idea of improving the chipped edge by rubbing the sharpened edge with another stone. Sharpening was discovered and the Neolithic Age began. (Rubbing of stones is one major difference between the New Stone Age and the preceding Old Stone Age.)

It was not long after the invention of the sharpened edge that man learned that sharpness is not a permanent state. He probably learned it that same afternoon, when he tried to cut his second tiger steak. Thus, the art of sharpening was forced on early man and has remained a necessity ever since.

1

At first, sharpening was simply a matter of rubbing one stone against another. Then as metals and metal alloys were discovered, sharpening became a matter of rubbing a stone against a metal. When the metals became harder, man searched until he found stones especially suited to sharpening. In fairly recent times, synthetic sharpening stones were developed — stones that are hard enough and abrasive enough to sharpen the hardest metals.

Today there are specific "stones" and stone shapes (as well as other tools) for properly sharpening every edged tool and every metal and alloy used for an edged tool. This bulletin will tell you the proper way to sharpen many common hand tools — chisels, various types of knives, shears, scissors, tin snips, hatchets, axes, mauls, auger bits, and saws.

Proper tool sharpening is a precision craft. You will need a lot of practice before you will achieve consistently good results. Practice, experiment, ruin a few practice blades, even shed a few tears of frustration — and then practice some more. Eventually you will master the craft of sharpening.

This bulletin will have much greater value for you if you watch the motions described here performed properly once or twice. Find someone who regularly sharpens tools — a local farmer, fireman, meatcutter, trapper, or even a professional tool sharpener — and watch how it is done. Then practice with this bulletin as your guide. And good luck!

The Cutting Edge

No edge remains sharp with use. The edge dulls as the metal wears. The sharper the edge, the more quickly it wears, and the more often it requires sharpening to maintain an ultrafine edge.

Corrosion is another enemy of a sharp edge. Visible rust prevents a knife from sliding smoothly through the substance being cut. There is also invisible corrosion, which can be caused by fruit juices attacking the metal blade. This is why when you cut something acidic, even with a stainless steel knife, it is good practice to wipe the knife dry immediately afterwards.

Just how thick must an edge be to be considered dull? This is a matter of application. A sharp knife would be quite dull when used as a razor. Technically, when an edge exceeds 1/200 (0.02) of an inch, it is pretty dull; but in general, a knife is too dull when it will not cut for you.

Metals

Ordinary steel is a mixture of iron and carbon. The more carbon, the harder the steel. The harder the carbon steel, the sharper the edge it can be given and will hold. Unfortunately, the harder carbon steel is made, the more brittle it becomes. Therefore, it is impractical to make an edged tool from the hardest carbon steel possible. For example, an ax made out of brittle steel would be very sharp, but you would lose a chunk of it the first time you hit a frozen knot or a stone. In addition, you would have a difficult time trying to hand-sharpen it in the field. Axes are, therefore, made from comparatively mild steel.

The solution to the problem of brittleness is toughness. This is the ability of a hard metal to give a little so that it does not break. Toughness is produced by tempering and adding exotic metals such as chromium, vanadium, molybdenum, tungsten, and nickel. Unfortunately, with the exception of nickel, all the exotic metals are expensive.

Stainless steel is made by the addition of chromium and nickel. The stainless steels that hold the best edge depend almost entirely on chromium for their resistance to corrosion. The less expensive steels, which resist corrosion much better, contain the less expensive, softer nickel. The alloy found best for cutlery is the so-called

"400" series of stainless alloys. The best in this series is "440–C" which has a 17-percent to 19-percent chromium content.

Commercial cutlery used by professional butchers and chefs are straight-carbon blades made from an alloy of steel that is primarily carbon and iron. The mix contains 50 to 80 parts of carbon to 1,000 parts of iron. Less carbon makes for a steel that is easily dulled. More carbon makes for a steel that is easily nicked and difficult to sharpen. Add sufficient carbon and you get steel that is almost as hard as a diamond and just as brittle. In any case, without the addition of chromium and/or nickel, these straight-carbon blades corrode, stain, and rust. They must be kept dry or oiled.

Bevels

The angle or bevel that forms the cutting edge of a tool is called its *edge bevel*. The edge bevel that you find on a tool (unless it has been altered by age or error) is that bevel best suited to the steel that makes up the tool and the way the tool is used. If you alter the edge bevel to make it longer and narrower, you weaken the edge. It will dull more quickly and chip more easily. If you shorten the bevel and broaden the angle, the cutting ability of the tool will be reduced. The angle formed by the edge bevels of common cutting tools ranges from 10 to 50 degrees. The sharper the angle, the better the tool cuts or slices, but the weaker the edge because there is less metal behind it. Here are some common edge bevel angles.

Razors	10 degrees
Pocket knives	15 degrees
Cutlery	25 to 35 degrees
Chopping edges	35 to 45 degrees
Mauls and wedges	50 degrees

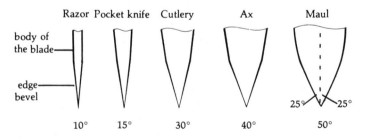

Typical edge bevel angles of various cutting tools. All are double bevels.

Basic Techniques

The process of sharpening any tool consists of restoring the original cutting edge(s) by removing a little metal. This is accomplished in two steps, which sometimes can be subdivided into a number of separate steps. The first step is called *beveling*, which some call grinding. The second step is called *honing*, or polishing, finishing, or stropping. With experience and the correct tools, both steps need not take more than five minutes for simple cutting edges, like knives and plane blades. Multiple blades, like saws, may require thirty minutes to an hour or more, depending on the number of teeth to be sharpened.

Beveling

Beveling reestablishes the original edge bevel angle of the tool. Just how much metal has to be removed depends on the nature of the tool and the amount of metal that has worn or broken away.

Assume that you are working on the edge of an old door, and you are planing away with vim and pleasure. Suddenly your plane strikes an old, unseen nail. A chip, perhaps 1/8 inch deep, breaks from the blade of the plane. You can, if you wish, continue planing, but the plane will leave a ridge with every pass. To enable the plane to cut smoothly and true again, you will have to remove sufficient metal from the edge of the blade to restore the full and original bevel.

Assume another condition. You are in the field and have neither the time nor the tool with which to sharpen your ax properly. Instead you just touch it up a little with a file. In a short while, there is no semblance of the original bevel; the edge is rounded. To return this edge to its original bevel a lot of metal has to be removed.

In both cases, and in similar instances where an edge has been terribly dulled or damaged, grinding is the only practical way to restore the bevel.

Grinding is accomplished with a coarse stone. You can place the tool in a vise or on your workbench and move the stone over the edge of the tool, making certain to hold the stone at the correct angle to the cutting edge at all times. Or you can place the stone on

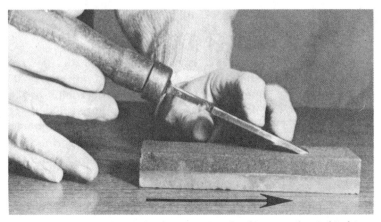

Basic position of tool and sharpening stone. In this example, a chisel is sharpened on a combination bench stone, coarse side up. Two hands are used to make certain the angle of the chisel blade against the stone remains the same. The arrow shows the direction in which the tool is moved. On the return stroke, little or no pressure is applied to the tool.

the bench and run the edge of the tool across the stone. In either case, it is a lot of work if there is a lot of metal to be removed.

The easier way to grind is to use a power grinder. There are several kinds. There is the old-fashioned whetstone, the modern bench grinder, and the grindstone mounted on an electric drill.

To use an old-fashioned whetstone, turn the grindstone with your hand or your foot and keep the edge of the tool pressed firmly against the edge of the revolving stone. Wear gloves and safety glasses when using a bench grinder, and take care not to apply too much pressure. Otherwise, you might overheat the edge of the tool, which will soften it. The tricky part here is getting the tool to pass over the grindstone evenly and at the same angle and pressure over the entire length of the blade. This is very hard to do freehand. If you can rig up some apparatus to rest the blade on at the proper angle, it makes the job much easier.

The drill-mounted grindstone is the least desirable arrangement because it is difficult to hold the edge of the wheel correctly against the edge of the tool. However, it is a lot easier than hand-grinding. The tool must be placed firmly in a vise. Again, you need to wear gloves and safety glasses. Apply little pressure and stop frequently to examine the edge of the tool.

When the grindstone is thicker than the width of the edge of the tool, and that edge is straight, maintaining the proper tool-to-wheel angle is no problem; just hold the tool steady. When the edge of the tool is wider than the thickness of the grindstone, hold the tool-to-wheel angle steady, and move the tool from side to side so that the stone touches all of the edge evenly. Avoid a swinging motion or your corners will become rounded. When the edge of the tool is curved, swing the tool in an arc, always holding the tool-to-stone angle steady.

Honing

When the original bevel has been restored with a fine-graded stone, the marks left by the fine-grit stone are removed by an even harder stone with a still finer grit. If you examine the bevel at this point, you will see that it is beginning to shine. The next step is honing, or stropping. Very simply, you polish the beveled edge with the rough side of the strop and then the smooth side. Five or ten strokes are all that are needed. For the ultimate in sharpness, the blade is then drawn across the palm of your hand a half dozen times. If you are not sharpening soft stainless steel, the edge should be sharp enough to cut a hair without bending it, or cut a sliver from your fingernail without pulling.

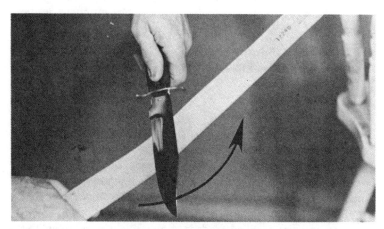

Stropping a knife on the back of a man's belt. The blade is drawn in a direction away from its edge; in the wrong direction, you would shave the belt.

Tools for Sharpening

Sharpening is the process of removing metal. For rapid metal removal, use a *stone*, natural or man-made, that consists of comparatively coarse abrasive particles or grains. The coarse abrasives leave a rough edge; so after using a "coarse" stone, follow with a second stone having very fine abrasive particles or grit. Instead of a stone, you might use a *file* to remove metal. Finally, use *leathers* for the final honing.

Stones

Stones and abrasives are graded by grit and hardness. They come in various shapes.

Grit. *Grit* refers to the size of the particles or grains that comprise the stone or abrasive. It is measured by the size of the smallest hole through which a particle of grit can pass. Grit ranges from 8 to 600, meaning the number of holes per lineal inch. The lower the grit number, the rougher the surface the stone produces; the finer the grit, the smoother the surface it produces; and the more slowly it cuts.

Here are some general guidelines you can follow to choose stones. If the stones you have do not carry grit numbers, you can safely follow the manufacturers' suggestions.

Fast metal removal	24 to 35 grit
Moderately rapid metal removal	36 to 55 grit
Coarse beveling	55 to 65 grit
Fine beveling	65 to 120 grit
Honing	120 to 200 plus grit

In a combination stone for sharpening axes and the like, a 35/75 stone would be about right. For sharpening chisels and planes, a 50/100 stone would be about right. For sharpening knives and similar sharp edges, you might select a 65/120 stone.

Grade. Hardness, called *grade* in commercial stones, refers to the strength of the bond between grains. The harder the stone, the longer it will last, the longer it will remain flat under use, and the finer the edge it will produce compared to a softer stone of identical grit size. Unfortunately, the harder the stone, the higher its cost, and the more likely it will shatter if dropped on a concrete floor. Usually the harder synthetic stones like aluminum oxide (which is sold under the tradenames India and Alundum) or silicon carbide (sold by the name Crystolon) are used for beveling. Natural stones, such as queer creek, soft Arkansas, or hard Arkansas, are used for honing.

Shapes. Wheel-shaped abrasives are known as *grindstones*. *Handstones* may be any size and shape and may even have a handle. *Bench stones* are rectangular with parallel surfaces and are designed to be placed on a workbench. *Slipstones* have flat surfaces plus curved edges. Long, thin sharpening stones, which may have round, square, or triangular cross sections, are called *sticks*.

Care. There are two schools of thought on caring for stones. One holds with oil, the other with water. The oil people soak their new stones overnight in 10-weight or 20-weight automotive oil (never vegetable or cooking oil). They add a few drops of oil to the stone every time they use it. When the stone becomes glazed, they clean it with alcohol, gasoline, or kerosene. The water people use their stones dry. When the pores of the stone clog up, they clean them

A piece of sandpaper wrapped around a block of wood serves as a makeshift replacement for a bench stone.

with warm soap and water and a scrub brush. I hold with the water people.

Files

Files are sometimes used instead of stones. You can remove more metal, stroke for stroke, with a file than with an equally coarse stone. Also, long, thin files are much stronger than long, thin stones and less likely to break in your hand. In the case of sharpening saws, files are the only practical tools to use. Stones are sometimes used to hone saw teeth, but never to bevel them.

Leathers

Leather is used for the final honing. If you can secure a barber's leather strop, fine. If not, you can make do with an unpainted leather belt. Or, you can purchase a length of strap leather from a hardware store. A piece two or more inches wide is best. A little neat's-foot oil on the leather every now and then will help preserve it and keep it soft.

Other Sharpening Tools

There are times when you do not have a sharpening stone at hand, and there are tools that are more easily and quickly sharpened with other devices. You can use sandpaper and field stones for grinding and steels for honing.

Sandpaper. Sandpaper is graded by grit size as are abrasive stones. However, for reasons unknown, sandpaper grit is coarser than abrasive grit. For example, for the same job that would require a 100-grit stone, you would use 200-grit paper (and still, you would not get the same smoothing effect).

To use sandpaper, either place the paper flat on your bench and bring the tool to the paper; or fasten the paper in a standard holder and bring the holder to the tool, just as you would use a handstone.

Power sanders. For an occasional rough-beveling job, you can use a sanding disk mounted on a drill motor. The larger drills are

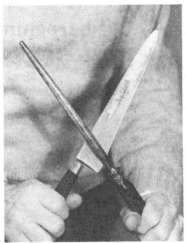

Honing with a steel. The tip of the edge of the knife is pressed against the steel (left). Then the knife and the steel are crossed, causing the steel to slide across the length of the edge of the knife (right). Repeat the operation a few times and you are ready to resume carving the roast.

preferable, as the motors have a slower speed. You can also use motor-driven belt sanders for sharpening. In all cases, wear protective glasses, as the belt tends to throw grains of sand and bits of metal. *Use a minimum of pressure;* it is easy to bear down too hard. If you force its edge into the paper, the tool may jerk out of your hands violently and fling the paper in your face. Several light passes do the best job.

Field stones. Any brick or stone that has one reasonably flat surface can be used for sharpening. A field stone or brick is used exactly as you would a sharpening stone.

Honing with steel. A steel is used to hone the edge of a carving knife after every three or four slices. It is a long, thin, round bar of steel. The steel is made of a harder alloy than the knife, and the surface has been roughened by tiny slits. In effect, the steel is a fine-toothed file. But a file is used in a drawing motion and is pulled away from the work, the steel is pushed against the knife edge.

Sharpening Techniques
for Individual Tools

Now that we have covered the basic terminology and equipment used with sharpening, it is time to reemphasize that proper tool sharpening is an art that takes time to master.

Approach each task carefully. If it seems that you will have difficulty holding the tool steady against the stone, rig up a guide to hold the tool at the proper angle. Maintaining the proper tool-to-stone angle is the whole secret of proper sharpening.

PLANE IRONS

Plane irons or blades are easy to sharpen because they have a single, straight bevel. The iron itself is flat. Only the cutting edge is beveled.

You will need a two-grit stone with a fine-grit side of 100 or more and a very steady hand or a guide for holding the blade. You can purchase a guide in a hardware shop, or make one yourself. In either case, the guide can be used for a number of tools.

A plane iron has been clamped in a homemade jig, the blade positioned in the jig so that the edge bevel is just right. Now the blade and jig can be pushed along the length of the stone several times, until the blade is sharpened.

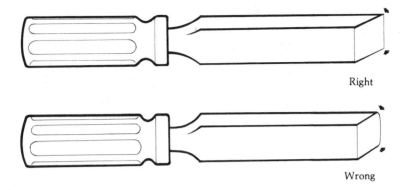

Right

Wrong

The end of the bevel must make a right angle with the side of the blade.

1. Remove and examine the blade. Remove whatever rust is present with steel wool. View the bevel in good light. The width of the bevel should be equal across the full width of the blade. The end of the bevel must make a right angle with the side of the blade. Note if there are any visible nicks more than 1/64 of an inch deep. If the bevel width is uneven, if the end of the steel is not square with the side, or if there are deep nicks, considerable metal must be removed. This is best done by grinding.

2. Use a wheel in the 55-grit to 65-grit range, 1-inch thick, and preferably thicker. (It is easier to grind an even and accurate bevel when the face of the wheel is as wide or wider than the tool to be ground.) Do not attempt to position the iron by hand alone; use a guide, making certain the guide is parallel to the face of the stone. Some craftsmen also tighten a pair of machinist's parallel clamps across the blade. Pressing the clamp edge against the guide keeps the blade at right angles to the face of the wheel.

If possible, restore the bevel to its original angle. If not, grind the edge back to 30 degrees. The angle is not critical, you can estimate it. Generally the angle is correct when the bevel is roughly twice the thickness of the plane iron blade.

Use little pressure and stop as soon as you have corrected the bevel — removed the nicks, evened the width of the bevel, and made it straight across. Remember, the bevel must be one flat surface.

3. The next step is coarse-beveling. Place the coarser side of the bench stone up. Fasten the blade in the guide. Check the angle by

making certain the bevel lies flat on the stone before you tighten the guide. Position the end of the blade at the end of the stone and push it forward along the length of the stone. (Dragging the blade produces a wire edge, a fine curl on the edge, which has to be removed.) Use little pressure and full strokes. Five or ten strokes should be sufficient. Examine the bevel. It should be a single, shiny surface.

4. Turn the stone over and with the tool still in the guide, give the blade five or so light strokes. If you wish, you can repeat this with a still finer-grit stone; but for most work, this is not necessary.

WOOD CHISELS

Old-time wood chisels have little or no bevel in their blade sections. But the blade is twice as thick as a plane iron. This makes for a very wide edge bevel, which may look like it is considerably less than 30 degrees, but rarely is. Modern wood chisels have shorter bodies with a more pronounced bevel to their blades. Still, you want the same 30-degree edge bevel on these tools. If someone, in error, has cut a second, shorter bevel on their edge, either you must grind or coarse-bevel the edge back to where it belongs. Wood chisels are then sharpened exactly the same as plane irons.

STRAIGHT-EDGED KNIVES

If the original edge bevel of the knife is clear enough to be followed, it is best to stick with the manufacturer's original angle. If the angle has been worn off or distorted by inaccurate sharpening, pick an angle from 25 to 35 degrees. For cutting soft things like bread, you want an acute angle. If you expect your knife to run into bone, you had best try for an angle of 35 degrees.

1. Hold the knife to the light. Ascertain whether there is a single-edge or a double-edge bevel. A single bevel means that you work from one side only. A double bevel means that you work both sides equally and that you split the angle. In other words, with a double bevel, if you are aiming for an edge bevel of 30 degrees, hold the knife at 15 degrees to the surface of the stone when you do each side.

Since the edge of the knife is longer than the width of the stone, to sharpen the knife you must hold the blade at the correct edge bevel angle, and as you move the knife forward along the stone, you must slide it sideways across the stone, so that the stone is brought to bear on the entire cutting edge of the knife.

2. Start at the near end of the coarse side of the bench stone. Hold the entire knife at the proper angle to the stone, its tip on the near end of the stone, the edge of the knife at a right angle to the stone. Move the knife toward the far end of the stone. As you do so, slide the knife diagonally across the stone. In this way you pass the entire edge of the knife across the stone. Keep the blade of the knife at right angles to the stone, and hold the flat of the knife at the same fixed angle to the stone. Repeat this action five or six times. If the knife has a double bevel, turn the knife over and rough-bevel the other side also.

3. Hold the knife edge up to the light. The bevel or bevels should be one smooth, narrow band without visible nicks or scratches. If not, rough-bevel some more. (This is where practice will tell.) When the bevels are smooth, turn the stone over and hone the knife exactly as you rough-beveled it.

4. For a still finer edge, strop the edge. Pull the knife edge toward you, across the rough side of the leather, four or five times on each bevel. Then turn the leather and pull the edge across the smooth side of the leather four or five times.

5. As an alternative to stropping, you can touch up the edge with a steel. Hold the steel by its handle and the knife by its handle.

Spread your hands apart. Touch the tip of the steel to the tip of the knife. Now, push the steel and knife together so that the steel slides across the knife edge, and the knife and steel cross near their handles. Do both bevel edges, if there are two. A few light passes of the steel are all that is needed.

STRAIGHT-EDGED POCKET KNIVES

Pocket knives with straight cutting edges can be sharpened exactly the same way as straight-edged cutlery knives. The only difference is the edge bevel. Pocket knives and similar small knives usually have an edge bevel of about 15 degrees.

In some instances the blade bevel and the edge bevel are one. In such cases, all you need do is place the flat of the blade against the stone and stroke just as you would a straight-edge knife. If the blade bevel is not the same as the edge bevel, you will have to make several test passes of the knife across the stone to establish the correct bevel angle. You can tell you have the correct angle by examining the blade after each trial pass. The width of the shiny metal exposed by the pass should line up with the line of the factory bevel or the bevel of a previous accurate sharpening.

When you have the correct angle, use your fingers to set and

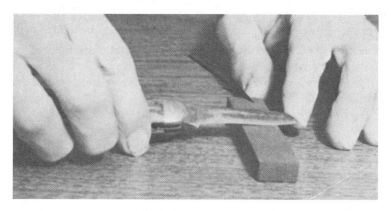

Sharpening a pocket knife. Since the edge bevel angle is very small, the blade lies almost flat against the surface of the stone. But the motion of the knife against the stone is the same as for a straight-edge cutlery knife (see p. 15). Here a small pocket stone is used in place of the larger bench stone.

hold the angle while you push the knife across the stone. Rough-bevel and hone both bevel angles as necessary.

DRAW KNIVES

Draw knives are large, straight-edged blades with a single bevel. There are two ways to sharpen them.

● Raise a bench stone on a block of wood. Then bevel the blade as suggested for a straight-edged knife blade. This procedure probably will give you the most uniform results.

or

● Put the draw knife in a vise. Bevel with a combination circular ax stone.

Since a draw knife cannot be made too sharp, it is advisable to hone draw knives as carefully as you would a fine knife.

CURVED-EDGED KNIVES

Sharpening curved edges is more difficult sharpening than straight edges. You have to turn the knife as you slide it across the stone. There is no simple jig that you can make for this movement, which means you need lots of good hand control and plenty of practice to produce a fine cutting edge.

1. Place the tip of the knife on the near end of the stone. Hold the body of the blade at its edge bevel angle to the stone. Tilt the body of the blade so that the edge bevel at the tip of the blade lies flat against the stone.

2. Push the knife away from you across the stone. As you do so, swing the handle of the knife around, away from you, so that the main body of the blade forms a right angle with the body of the stone. At the same time, slide the knife sideways across the stone. What you are doing is making a sweeping, curving motion, a motion that keeps the edge bevel of the blade flat on the stone and at the same time moves the bevel across the stone.

3. When you have coarse-beveled both edge bevels, repeat the process with the fine side of the bench stone.

4. If you wish, go on to a finer stone still; then strop the blade with a leather.

Sharpening a curved-edged knife. The tip of the blade is held against one end of the stone. The blade body is held at an angle to the stone. The blade is lifted until the edge bevel at the tip of the blade lies flat against the stone (left). As you push the knife forward against the stone, swing the knife across the stone. Shown here (right) is the finishing position. To continue sharpening, lift the blade and reposition it as shown on the left.

HUNTING KNIVES

Hunting knives differ from curved-edged, cutlery knives only in the thickness of their blades and their edge bevels. Since hunting knives are used primarily for dressing game, there is a good chance they will strike bone. Therefore, their edge bevels are designed to be on the order of 30 to 35 degrees. Usually, their cutting edges are double-beveled.

Sharpen hunting knives just as you would a curved-edge knife. Pay special attention to the tip; it is important that it be sharp for making the entering cut.

BRUSH KNIVES

Brush knives are used when and where there is no need for the heavier bush ax — and sickles, scythes, or grass hooks will not do. Brush knives include machetes, which have fairly straight cutting edges, and bolo knives, which have curved, scimitar-shaped cutting edges.

Although most of these knives come sharpened to an edge bevel of 24 degrees to 30 degrees, this bush hacker believes a 30-degree to 35-degree cutting edge to be preferable. The more acute cutting edge becomes dull much too quickly.

When sharpening a machete, treat it just as you would any straight cutting edge. You can ignore the curved end of the blade because that portion of the blade is rarely used for cutting. However, after repeated sharpenings, you must rough-bevel the end of the blade to keep the cutting edge straight.

Bolo knives are sharpened the same way as curved-edged knives. The only difference is that the edge bevel should be 30 to 35 degrees, as suggested for the machete. From an economy of labor point of view, you do not have to sharpen the blade all the way out to its tip. Like the machete, the end of the bolo knife does not do much cutting.

GOUGES

A gouge is a wood chisel with a semitubular working end. Generally, the bevel is on the outside of the curve just as the bevel on a wood chisel is on the portion of the steel that rides on the wood.

The edge bevel angle is generally around 30 degrees. However, since it follows a curve, sharpening cannot be done in the usual way. Each method that follows can be used (or try a combination of both).

• Bevel the edge of the tool by holding the gouge at the correct edge bevel angle to a bench stone; hold the tool handle high so that the edge bevel rests on the surface of the stone. Then rotate the entire tool along its length as you maintain the proper edge bevel angle. This is first done against the coarse side of the stone; then the edge is honed on the fine-grit side of the stone.

or

• The alternate method is to hold the gouge against the stone at its bevel angle, the way you would hold a wood chisel. Push the gouge forward — very lightly — against the stone. With each stroke, rotate the tool slightly so that the entire bevel is sharpened.

STRAIGHT-EDGED HATCHETS AND AXES

The edge bevels of hatchets and axes are treated exactly like straight-edge knife bevels. The only difference lies in the quantity of metal removed.

1. Examine the cutting edge. If it has been chipped or incorrectly sharpened, you will have to reshape the edge bevel. You can do this with a bench stone or a grindstone. In the latter case, take care not to apply so much pressure the metal is overheated and softened.

2. If you have used a grindstone, rework the bevels on the rough side of a bench stone. Bear in mind the angle you want. Spend sufficient time to make the edge bevel one single smooth band. If you have been rough-beveling with a bench stone, just make certain you reach the same condition before you go on to honing.

3. Next the bevels are honed. Just how much honing and the grit of the stone to use depends on how sharp you want your hatchet or ax.

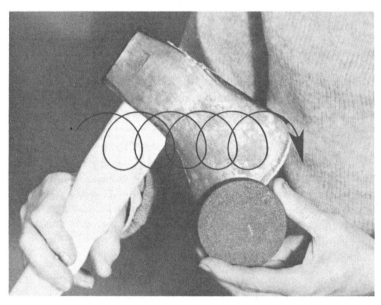

Using a round handstone to sharpen an ax. The stone is rubbed in a circular motion against the edge of the ax.

HATCHETS, AXES, AND MAULS

The difference between a hatchet, ax, and maul from a sharpening point of view lies entirely in their cutting edges. The hatchet, which is the lightest of the three tools, has a cutting edge beveled from 30 to 36 degrees. Very often it is made as sharp as a knife. An ax is usually beveled at 36 to 46 degrees. The bevel may be *cannell*, which means rounded. Usually, the edge is not honed because a honed edge will soon blunt when the ax is pounded into wood. Mauls are usually cannell-beveled to an angle of 50 degrees. Mauls are not designed for cutting, but for splitting. Weighing 6 to 8 pounds at their head, they are a combination wedge and sledgehammer.

CURVED-EDGED HATCHETS AND AXES

1. Examine the cutting edge. Rough-bevel it down to where it should be. But now, instead of simply moving the ax or hatchet straight across the stone or wheel, you have to swing the handle of the tool so that the head passes against the stone in an arc that conforms to the curve of the cutting edge. This requires a steady hand, a good eye, and lots of practice.

2. Rough-bevel the edge as required; then hone the edge bevels to whatever degree of sharpness you wish.

Field sharpening hatchets and axes. The round handstone with its two grits is probably the easiest tool to use for field sharpening hatchets, axes, and the like. Since it is round, it is easily carried.

To use the round handstone, simply press it against the edge bevel and work the stone in a circle, taking care to work it evenly against the entire surface of the edge bevel. Hone with the finer-grit side of the stone.

You will get much faster cutting action sharpening with a file — if you use both hands to develop the necessary pressure. You cannot do this with a file stone because you might crack it if you press down on its ends while its center is over the ax edge. To use a file, grip the tool head between your knees at a comfortable

CANNELL EDGES

The advantages of a cannell, or rounded, edge is that it stands up to abuse much better than a straight edge. On the other hand, the cannell edge tends to retard the penetration of the tool through the material it is cutting. This is why it is limited mainly to chopping tools.

To form a cannell edge, proceed as directed for sharpening an ax or similar tool that has an edge bevel of 35 degrees or more. This done, note that the edge bevels form a very fine edge — the cutting edge — where they meet. Note also that the bevels form angles with the sides of the tools. To round off these angles and change the bevel edge to a rounded edge, these side angles must be removed. This can be done by changing the angle of the tool blade against the stone or file several times as you work the steel against the stone or file.

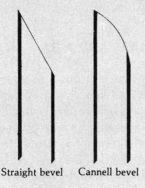

Straight bevel   Cannell bevel

Bevels can be straight or rounded (cannelled). A rounded edge is less likely to be nicked by rocks or hard objects.

angle. Hold the file by its two ends, maintaining the correct edge bevel angle, and pull the file against the cutting edge.

MAULS

1. Rough-bevel the edge down to where it should be.
2. Using a coarse, 60-grit or so handstone, or a 100-grit or so grindstone, remove the rough-bevel marks from the edge bevel of the maul. When the edge bevels feel smooth, the job is done. A knife edge usually is not desired on a maul.

SCYTHES

Stand the scythe on the end of its handle, with the blade in a horizontal position. Place the stone against the blade so that the stone touches both the backbone of the blade and the cutting edge. Then, with one graceful sweep, draw the stone across the full length of the blade. The thickness of the backbone is such that you will secure the correct edge bevel. Generally, scythes have two bevels of 10 degrees each, making for a 20-degree cutting edge.

SICKLES

Generally, a sickle has a single bevel. Some sickles are made with a backbone, which you can use as a beveling guide, as suggested for sharpening scythes. Others have no backbone; in such cases you must gauge the bevel by eye. The sharpening stone is pushed along the blade, just as with a scythe.

Sharpening a scythe using a bar-shaped stone. The scythe rests on the end of its handle. The stone is placed against the blade so that the stone touches both the backbone of the blade and its cutting edge. The stone is drawn along the full length of the blade in one smooth motion.

SCYTHES, SICKLES, AND BUSH AXES OR HOOKS

These tools have their cutting edges on the inside of the blade arc, which makes them easier to sharpen than bolo knives and other tools that have their sharpened edges on the outside of the arc. However, inner-arc cutting tools are much more difficult to edge on a grinding wheel.

You will need a bar-shaped stone for this task. These stones are sometimes called scythe or sickle stones and may have an oval cross section that is tapered towards the ends of the stone. Some have handles. Generally a single, medium-grit stone is used. No effort is made to hone these edges. It is not worth the trouble because the edges dull too quickly. The usual practice is to carry a stone in one's pocket and sharpen the scythe or sickle frequently. It is a good excuse to stop working and rest a moment.

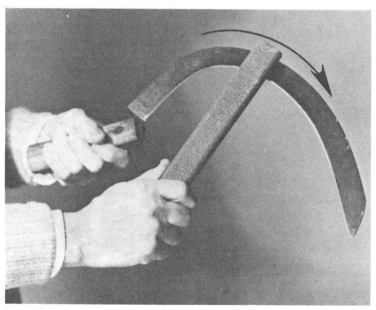

Sharpening a sickle. The motion is the same as for a scythe (p. 23) — smooth, even strokes along the length of the blade.

Sharpening a bush hook. The same swinging stroke is used on a sickle and a scythe.

BUSH AXES OR HOOKS

The body of this tool is much thicker than the bodies of the other hooked tools. This does not change the sharpening process. It just means that there is a lot more metal to remove when the edge is nicked and battered. Generally, bush axes have two bevels totaling in the range of 40 degrees to 50 degrees. Most often the cutting edge is cannelled.

The same stone and method are used to restore the cutting edge on this tool as are suggested for the scythe and sickle. However, should you need to grind a badly nicked edge, you will find a half-round file much more useful than a stone. If you want to use a power grindstone you will need a dual-cone stone designed for the purpose.

SCISSORS

Scissors cut as the edges of the two blades come together and pass closely across each other. If you examine the cutting edges you will see that they have been ground to a bevel of about 80 degrees.

It is these edges that do the cutting. When these edges become rounded with wear, the scissors fail to cut properly. It is a simple matter to resharpen these edges. Never sharpen the insides of the blades, the surfaces that meet. This would remove metal so that the surfaces would no longer touch, and the scissors would no longer cut. Only sharpen the existing beveled edges.

1. Open the scissors and place one blade in a vise, cutting edge up.
2. Place a medium-grit stone atop the cutting edge. Pull or push the stone directly across the blade, taking care to hold the stone parallel to the cutting edge. Repeat this operation over the entire blade length.
3. Do the same to the other blade edge.
4. Hone to remove any wire edges that may form.

SHEARS AND TIN SNIPS

Shears and tin snips are both forms of scissors — differing only in the size and thickness of their blades. If you examine the snips closely, you will see the edge bevels. Just work the stone across these bevels, taking care to hold to the original angle.

Some shears have a serrated-blade edge as well as a simple bevel-edge blade. Handle the straight-bevel edge just as you would any straight edge. The edge bevel angle is usually about 35 degrees. Finish up with a 100-grit stone. Next, examine the serrated edge. Note that the edge itself is not serrated but ground at an angle similar to that of a scissor — about 80 degrees to the flat side of the blade. Ignore the serrations and work on this flat, narrow bevel just as you would on an ordinary scissor blade.

COMPOUND TIN SNIPS

If you examine the blades of compound tin snips, you will see that the edge bevel is a continuous curve that wraps around the blade terminating at the flat side of the blade. To sharpen these tools you need to take the blades apart. Then follow the curve with

Using a small stone to sharpen a pair of tin snips. Hold the stone flat against the edge bevel and push the stone across the blade.

a fine-grit stone, pushing the stone along the edge bevel from the curve towards the flat of the blade.

SNAP-CUT SHEARS

Snap-cut shears cut by the action of a steel knife striking against a brass anvil. If you examine the blade you will see a very narrow, double-edge bevel of about 30 degrees. To sharpen, touch these edges up with a fine-grit stone. Be careful to bevel each side of the blade equally. If the bevel is skewed, it will not strike the anvil properly, and the cutting action will be greatly reduced.

AUGER BITS

An auger bit has a screw that acts to pull the bit against the wood. As the bit is turned, two spurs projecting forward cut a circle in the wood. Two flat cutting edges remove the wood from within the circle cut by the spurs. Sharpening is not difficult but it must be done carefully if the bit is to cut smoothly and evenly.

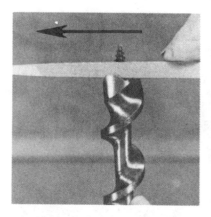
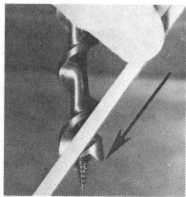

Sharpening an auger bit. First the inside edges of one spur are sharp-
ened (left). Then the edges of the other spur are sharpened. Make sure
you do not rub the file against the screw head. Then the cutting edges
are sharpened (right). Note carefully the relation of the file to the cutting
edge. Only the inside of the cutting edge should be sharpened.

1. Examine the spurs. With a fine file, an auger-bit stone, or any small abrasive stick, touch up the edge bevels on the two spurs. Work from the inside only. Take care not to bevel one spur more than the other, or to reduce the height of one spur in relation to the other. This done, carefully remove any wire edges that may have formed. Never sharpen these spurs from the outside.

2. Position the bit point down. Use the same stone or file to edge-bevel the two cutting edges. 'Apply the stone or file to the upper side of these cutting edges only. Think of them as two tiny planes going round and round in a circle. Remove whatever wire edges may have formed.

3. Go over all the cutting edges with a fine stone to hone them.

CURVED-BLADED PRUNING SHEARS

Curved-bladed pruning shears, lopping shears, and tree trimmers have one curved, beveled blade that works against a flat-surfaced hook or bar. Although the edge of this bar or hook is not sharpened, its edge has to be at right angles to the beveled blade.

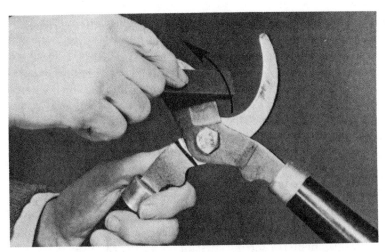

Sharpening a pair of curved-bladed pruning shears. A small stone is swung along the curved edge of the blade. The edge bevel is very narrow and has an angle of about 50 degrees; do not alter it.

1. Open the shears as far as they will go. Place the shears in a vise or prop against a bar or fence.

2. To bevel, swing a coarse stone along the curved edge of the blade. Note that the edge bevel is very narrow and angled at about 50 degrees.

3. Run a bar stone along the inside curve of the hook so as to make its edges perfectly square and clean.

HANDSAWS

1. The first step is leveling the height of the teeth. Place the saw, teeth up, in a saw vise, or improvise one from an ordinary vise and two strips of wood. Run a flat file down the length of the saw, holding the file flat with its length on top of the teeth. If all the teeth are the same height, the file will leave a shiny mark on all of them. If some are shorter, file the high teeth down. But do not file the teeth down to the height of a broken tooth; you'll end up with no teeth at all. Now, some of the teeth will have flat tops. The next step will restore the triangular shape to the teeth.

2. Select a triangular file twice as thick as the depth of each gullet (space between teeth). With the saw still in the vise, note that the leading edge of the teeth on ripsaws is perfectly vertical; the leading edge of teeth on crosscut saws is usually angled at about 14 degrees. With the file held horizontally, follow the angle of the end, unworn teeth. Work with steady, forward-cutting strokes and apply pressure as you move the file forward only. Don't worry about the constant 60 degrees between teeth. The triangular file takes care of that. On crosscut saws, file every other tooth at the proper angle, then file the remaining teeth in the opposite direction. Stop filing when you have brought the top of each tooth to a point.

3. Next, the teeth have to be set. This consists of bending the top halves of each tooth to the side for a distance equal to approximately the thickness of the saw blade. Crosscut saws should be set to each side about 1/4 the thickness of the blade; ripsaws are set 1/3 the thickness of the blade. Bend direction alternates from tooth to tooth. Setting causes the saw's teeth to cut a slot (kerf) twice as wide as the blade itself. A saw with unset teeth (they straighten with use) binds. Do not try to set a saw with hairline cracks near the teeth; they will crack under pressure.

The best way to set saw teeth is to use one of the tooth-setting

---

SHARPENING SAWS

The Egyptians invented the saw some four thousand years ago, shortly after they began to work with copper. Like the method they used to build the pyramids, the method they used to keep their copper saws sharp remains a mystery. It is difficult enough to keep a high-steel saw sharp. Imagine keeping a copper saw sharp.

Correctly sharpened saws are a pleasure to work with. They cut true, fast, and easily. Unfortunately, saw sharpening is still a tedious task that requires considerable care. Four steps are involved.

- *Leveling*, sometimes called jointing. This involves bringing all the teeth to the same height.
- *Tooth shaping*, sometimes called gumming or gullet filing.
- *Setting*, which consists of angling the top halves of each tooth.
- *Sharpening*, which is our old friend, edge-beveling.

Using a pair of pliers to set the teeth of a handsaw. The bend direction alternates with each tooth. Be careful not to bend the teeth too far, or they will break off.

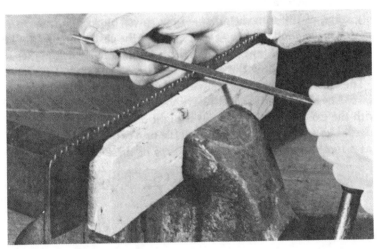

Sharpening a ripsaw. File straight across the saw blade. Apply light strokes to each tooth to achieve uniform results.

jigs available in most hardware shops. The second best method is to bend the teeth with the corner of a pair of pliers. Use the angle of the pliers as a guide to the angle at which you set each tooth. The second best method is far inferior to the first method, but it is a heck of a lot better than nothing. Do not overbend. Saw teeth break easily.

4. The last step is sharpening. To sharpen a ripsaw, file straight across the saw blade. To sharpen a crosscut saw, you have to hold

the file horizontal and at an angle that will permit the file to sharpen (or bevel) the leading edge of one tooth and the trailing edge of another. The file is held at an angle of 45 to 60 degrees, depending on how the teeth were originally beveled. Do not file too much, as doing so will shorten the tooth you are beveling. Use light strokes and apply the same number of strokes to each tooth for uniform results. There are guides made for this job, but it is not too difficult to do without a guide if you work carefully. Start with a new file and be prepared to discard it after sharpening just one average-size handsaw.

TIMBER SAWS

Timber saws include all saws with unevenly spaced teeth or teeth in groups of differing heights — bow saws, bucksaws, two-man crosscut saws, and the like. These saws are the easiest of all saws to sharpen. There are fewer teeth and they are large, which makes it easy to see and follow the original bevel.

The crosscut and ripsaw teeth are filed as suggested for the handsaws. The shorter, raker teeth have V-shaped tops. You have to go with the existing angles and file straight down so as to restore the edges. Use an 8-inch or 10-inch mill file or a cantsaw file. The latter has a flat V-shape that just fits the tops of these teeth.